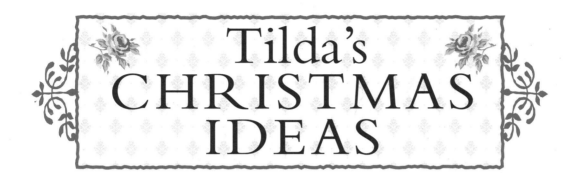

Tilda's
CHRISTMAS
IDEAS

A DAVID & CHARLES BOOK

Copyright © Tone Finnanger 2010
Originally published in Norway as *Tildas Juleideer*

First published in the UK in 2010 by David & Charles
Reprinted in 2010
David & Charles is an F+W Media Inc. company
4700 East Galbraith Road
Cincinnati, OH 45236

A catalogue record for this book is available from the
British Library.

ISBN-13: 978-0-7153-3865-0 paperback
ISBN-10: 0-7153-3865-X paperback

Printed in the UK by Butler, Tanner & Dennis
for David & Charles
Brunel House, Newton Abbot, Devon

Stylist Ingrid Skaansar
Photography Ragnar Hartvig

David & Charles publish high quality books on
a wide range of subjects.
For more great book ideas visit: **www.rucraft.co.uk**

Magical Christmas

Christmas is a truly magical time. It is a day that we spend the year looking forward to, whether we are young or just young-at-heart. Often the build-up can be even more fun than the big day itself, so to make the most of this energy and anticipation, we should start our preparations early. For many of us, this means making things ourselves, such as gifts, decorations and cakes. Craft and sewing are such perfect activities to fill the months leading up to Christmas.

In my world, creativity and making are a large part of everyday life, and I know how lucky I am. Twice a year, we produce a new collection of Tilda products, many of which I use in the books. However, I have also had lots of ideas for this season's new collection which we have not had time to produce a book for, so we've put together some great new projects for you here in this booklet.

As a designer, I'm coming up with new ideas all the time and I first had the idea to create a booklet to go with the new collections some time ago. We've now managed to make it a reality with this wonderful collection of gifts and keepsakes, of which I am really proud.

We've used new fabrics in all of these projects, but feel free to use different fabrics if you prefer, or a combination of old and new to suit your own style. The real value is in the design itself.

Enjoy!

Tone Finnanger

Contents

Materials

We've used Tilda fabric, buttons and ribbons to make the projects in this booklet. Tilda products are designed by Tone Finnanger and produced and distributed by Panduro Hobby.

Tilda products can be found at **www.pandurohobby.co.uk**

Read more about Tilda at **www.tildasworld.com**

Techniques

HAIR
Insert pins in the forehead, crown and over the back of the centre of the head. Also insert a pin on each side of the head. Wind on the hair, back and forth between the pins on each side and between the pins along the centre, see Figure A. When the head is covered, tack the hair in place and remove the pins. Attach a small bunch of hair to each side of the head, see Figure B.

A
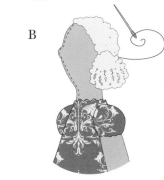

FACES
We recommend that you add the hair before marking the eyes to ensure they are correctly positioned. Insert pins into the head to check where the eyes should be. Remove the pins. Use the eye tool from the Tilda Face Painting set (ref. no. 713400) or make the eyes by dipping the head of a pin in some black paint and pressing onto the face where you have made the holes. Make rosy cheeks by applying some lipstick or blusher with a dry brush, after the eyes have dried.

B

EMBROIDERY
The pattern for the rose can be found on page 33. Hold the fabrics, with the pattern underneath, up against a window or light box so that the pattern shows through. Trace the pattern with a disappearing marker or a thin black pencil. If desired, iron thin fusible interfacing against the wrong side of the fabric where the rose will be embroidered, if the fabric is very thin. Use the embroidery yarn with all strands to fill the parts of the rose with the smallest possible stitches, see Figure C.

C
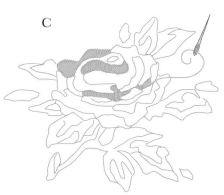

USING ILLUSTRATIONS
Illustrations of the wings in two sizes, the paper drum and the sign for the angels can be found on pages 46–47. Copy the design onto card or thick paper using a colour photocopier, or scan into your computer and print out. Alternatively copy or print the design onto ordinary paper and then glue it onto card. Cut out the parts and follow the instructions.

SEWING

Avoid cutting out the figure beforehand unless it is absolutely necessary. Fold the fabric double, right sides facing, and transfer the pattern onto it. Mark any openings for reversing indicated on the pattern. Sew carefully and evenly along the marked lines, using a stitch length of 1.5–2mm (⅝ – ¾ in).

CUTTING OUT

Cut out the figure with a narrow seam allowance, 3–4mm (⅛ in) is ideal. Extra seam allowance is required at the reversing sections of approximately 7–8mm (⅜ in). Snip incisions in the seam at the bends.

REVERSING

Use a florist's stick to help you with reversing. As a rule, use the blunt end, though the pointed end can be used carefully for small details. To avoid piercing the fabric, just cut off the top millimetre of the tip. Long, thin pieces such as legs can be turned inside out by pressing the blunt end against the foot, see Figure A. Starting at the foot, pull the leg over the stick, see Figure B. Continue to pull the leg over the stick until the foot appears at the top. Holding the foot, pull the rest of the leg over until it is completely turned right side out, see Figure C. Turn the arms in the same way.

STUFFING

Fold in the extra seam allowance along the opening in the seam, with the exception of the legs for the Santas and angels, where the seam allowance is tucked into the body and should not therefore be folded in. Iron the figure.

   When stuffing, use your finger to push the stuffing as far as you can, and then use a pen or a wooden stick to push into the parts you cannot reach. If the implement is too thin it will just push through the stuffing.

   Push the stuffing loosely into the figure and try to avoid over-filling it, which will cause lumps to form. Add stuffing to each section until full and continue to add stuffing until you have a perfectly formed figure. Then sew up the openings neatly.

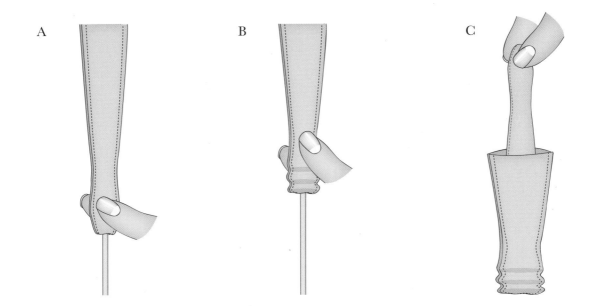

A   B   C

Santas

Patterns can be found on pages 43–45

YOU WILL NEED
Tilda skin fabric
Red fabric for the hat, arms and trousers
Fabric for the legs and coat
White velvet ribbon to decorate the coat
White Tilda hair for the beard
White embroidery yarn for the hat and coat
Tilda figure stand (optional)
Stuffing
Drum, see page 11
Ice skates, see page 22

HOW TO MAKE
Note that the patterns for the Santa body and coat are divided up to enable them to fit onto the pattern sheet. Sew the fabric pieces together so the dashed lines between A–A and B–B line up.

BODY
Sew together a piece of skin fabric that is large enough for the body and a piece of red fabric large enough for the hat, so that the join between the two is roughly as marked by the dashed line in the pattern.

Make the opposite piece in the same way. Place one piece on top of the other and ensure that both seams between hat and body line up. Copy the body as shown in the pattern and sew around, see Figure A. Cut out and fold inside out, then iron and stuff the body using a wooden stick to help.

Fold the fabric for the arms and legs, line up the edges and transfer the patterns. Sew around and cut out. Fold inside out, using a wooden stick to help for the narrow parts. Iron and fill the limbs.

Insert the legs in the opening of the body and tack it closed.

Tack and pull the thread tight at the opening on the arms at each end. Tack in place, just under the neck, see Figure B.

TROUSERS
Note that the trouser pattern is marked 'double fold' and must be double. Cut out two trouser parts, place one on top of the other, line up the edges and sew the crotch seams on both sides, see Figure C.

Fold the trousers in the opposite direction and stitch the legs together to form two trouser legs, see Figure D. Fold the trousers inside out and fold in the seam allowance at the openings before ironing the trousers. Place the trousers on the figure and attach with a few stitches at the waist. Tack around the leg openings and gather the trouser legs, see Figure E.

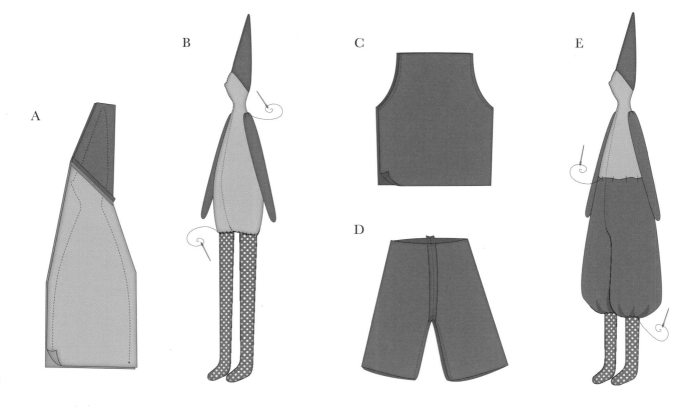

F

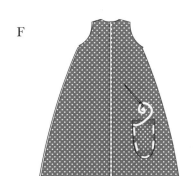

G

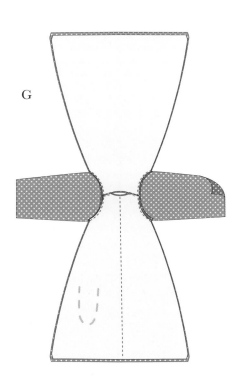

COAT

Cut out the two coat parts and two sleeves. Note that the large coat parts are marked 'double fold' and should be double.

Cut out two large coat pieces of thick fusible interfacing and iron onto the back of the fabric pieces. The sleeves do not require interfacing. Fold the fabric for the pocket and line up the edges. Copy the pattern for the pocket and sew around it. Cut a fold opening in one fabric layer as shown in the pattern. Fold inside out and iron the pocket.

Sew a velvet ribbon along the middle of the coat and attach as shown in the pattern. Sew on with large stitches in white embroidery yarn, see Figure F. Place one coat piece on top of the other and sew together at the shoulders. Fold out the parts and sew on the sleeves, see Figure G.

Fold the coat double and sew the sleeves together on each side, see Figure H. Cut off any excess seam allowance and snip incisions along the seam under each sleeve. Fold the coat inside out and iron. Fold in the seam allowance for each sleeve and hem the seam allowance at the base of the coat.

Tear 3cm (1¾ in) wide fabric strips from the dotted fabric and sew together to make a strip 140cm (56in) long.

Using large stitches, use a sewing machine to sew along the centre of the strip. Carefully pull at the strip by tugging the stitch underneath at each end until it is the same length as the bottom edge of the coat, see Figure I. Sew the strip around the base as a frill, then place the coat on the figure. Sew around and pull tight on the sleeves around each hand.

H

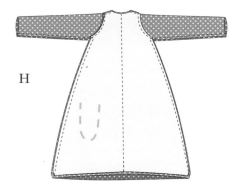

I

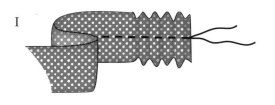

HAT AND BEARD

Fold the fabric for the ear warmers for the hat double. Transfer the pattern, sew around and cut out. Fold inside out and iron. Sew a decorative stitch with white embroidery yarn around the bottom edge. Tack on the ear warmers around the Santa's head, see Figure J.

Insert some hair under the edge of the hat, on each side of the head. Make a bunch of hair for the beard by winding Tilda hair around your hand and tying at one end. Tack the beard under the nose and up the sides of the face to join the hair. Attach the ends of the beard in the coat with a few stitches.

FACE AND BOWS

Cut four pieces of velvet ribbon, each measuring 8cm (3¼ in). Make four small bows by folding the ribbon as shown in Figure K. Tie some thread around the middle of the bows, see Figure L.

Attach the first bow approximately 2cm (¾ in) below the beard and distribute the rest of the bows evenly below the first. Make the face as described on page 4, trying not to get any rouge on the beard.

FINISHING TOUCHES

Attach the Santa to the figure stand by making holes in the body and inserting the stick until the legs are approximately 1cm (⅜ in) from the bottom of the stick. Glue the stick in the base and glue the legs to the stick if desired.

Make the drum as described on page 11. The drumsticks should be 8cm (3¼ in) long. Sharpen one end and glue on a wooden ball. Glue the drumstick to the pocket, hang the drum around the neck and glue one hand to the drumstick.

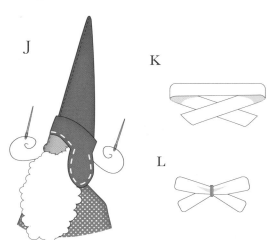

J

K

L

Pattern can be found on
pages 46–47

YOU WILL NEED
Photocopier
Paper or card
Ribbon
Double-sided tape
Stuffing

HOW TO MAKE
Transfer the drum pattern as
described on page 4, then cut out
all parts of the drum. Cut incisions
around the base and top of the
drum. Shape a cylinder from the
white part and fix with double-sided
tape, see Figure A.

Attach double-sided tape around
the edge at the top and bottom of
the cylinder. Attach the base to the
cylinder by sticking the flaps to the
double-sided tape. Stuff the drum
before attaching the top in the
same way.

Attach a 32cm (12 ¾ in)
length of red checked ribbon with
double-sided tape as a hanger, see
Figure B. Finally, glue the drum-
patterned piece around the cylinder,
see Figure C.

To make the drumsticks, see
page 10.

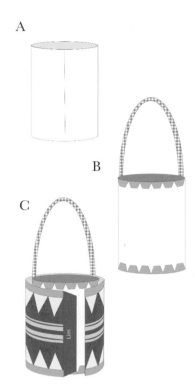

A

B

C

Pixies

Patterns can be found on pages 40–42

YOU WILL NEED

Tilda skin fabric
Fabric for the hat, legs and skirt
Decorative ribbon
Tilda hair
Embroidery yarn for the rose
Stuffing
Tilda figure stand (optional)

HOW TO MAKE

Note that the pattern for the Pixie bodies is split up to fit on the pattern page. Put the parts together so that the dashed lines between A–A and B–B line up.

Sew the body using the same method as for the body on page 6, but using the pattern on page 36. Sew the arms, legs and skirt in the same way as the Angels on page 25.

Stitch the rose and paint the face, referring to page 4 for instructions. Attach some hair along the edges of the hat and put a wind of hair on each side of the head.

Attach the Santa to the figure stand by making holes in the body and inserting the stick until the legs are approximately 1cm (³⁄₈ in) from the bottom of the stick. Glue the stick in the base and glue the legs to the stick if desired.

Baubles

Patterns can be found on pages 33–34

YOU WILL NEED
Various fabrics
Decorative ribbons
Hanging ribbon
Metal rings for hanging
Fusible interfacing
Stuffing

HOW TO MAKE
Note that the pattern comes in two different sizes. For the larger bauble, use a metal ring approximately 1.4cm (⅝ in) in size. For the smaller bauble, use a metal ring approximately 1cm (⅜ in) in size.

The back of the baubles is made using plain fabric so that you can make a simple opening. If you would like both sides to have patterned fabric, the opening will need to be in the seam around the bauble.

Sew the two fabrics together as shown in the pattern and iron fusible interfacing onto the back of the joined fabrics. Sew on your chosen ribbons and cut pieces of the backing fabric that holds half the pattern and has plenty of seam allowance.

Put the pieces together with printed sides facing each other. Sew together one side leaving an opening in the middle for reversing, see Figure A. Put the front and back with printed sides facing each other, transfer the pattern and sew around, see Figure B.

Cut out the bauble and cut incisions where the seams bend around. Turn right side out and iron. Stuff the bauble, pushing the filling against the seam before stuffing the rest, then steam iron to achieve an even shape. Attach the ring to the back of the bauble so that half of the ring goes through the fabric to the front. Attach ribbon to the ring to hang.

A

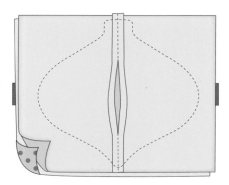

B

15

Patterns can be found on page 39

YOU WILL NEED
Cake tray with glass lid
Fabric for the body
Florist's stick
Paints for the noses
Buttons, ribbons and a decorative sign
Stuffing

HOW TO MAKE
BODY
Double fold a piece of fabric large enough for the snowman pattern. Note that the corners that turn in and create the base should be open in addition to the turn opening.

Sew around the snowman, see Figure A, then cut it out. Fold out and sew the bottom corners so that the seams are on top of each other to create a base, see Figure B. Turn out, iron and stuff the snowman then stitch the openings.

Make small noses by cutting a florist's stick into a short stub. Cut off the top to get a small nose and decorate using terracotta paint. Make the face as shown on page 4 and glue on the nose.

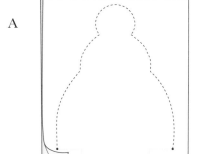

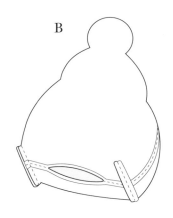

DECORATIONS

Tie a piece of ribbon around the neck as a scarf and attach buttons running down the centre of the body. Make the wings as shown on page 4 and glue them onto the figure. Glue a pom-pom to each side of the head to make ear warmers. Form a wire bow and attach in the pom-pom on each side. Glue the required number of snowmen to the cake tray, making sure they will all fit under the glass lid. Add some stuffing around the base as snow. Finish off by cutting out a sign in an L-shaped piece of card and fastening at the bottom.

SNOWMAN CANDLESTICKS

Create a snowman, following the instructions above, but leave the turn opening open. Using a glue gun, apply glue generously to the candleholder and insert it into the opening in the base. The snowman can now be attached to a strong branch of your Christmas tree.

Candy Cones

Patterns can be found on page 45

YOU WILL NEED

Fabric for cones and lining
Fusible interfacing
Decorative ribbon
Wire for hanging

HOW TO MAKE

Cut the fabric, fusible interfacing
and lining according to the
pattern. Iron Vlieseline onto the
back of the fabric, fold the fabric
and sew along the bow-shaped
edge, see Figure A.

Fold the cone the opposite way,
printed side by printed side and
sew along the open side, leaving
a turn opening in the lining, see
Figure B. Cut off any excess seam
allowance and turn right side out.
Push the lining inside the cone
and iron.

Cut a piece of wire, approximately
30–40cm (12–16in) long and put
the ends through the fabric on
each side of the cone. Tie the
ends of the wire around the rest
of the wire to make sure they are
fastened, as shown in the picture.
Glue or sew on your chosen ribbon.

A

B

Ice Skates

Patterns can be found on pages 32–34

YOU WILL NEED
Fabric for the ice skate and lining
Fusible interfacing
Tilda plywood ice skates
Decorative ribbon
Embroidery yarn for the rose and to
attach the boot
Wire (optional)

HOW TO MAKE
Cut out the entire ice skate shape
twice in your chosen fabric, lining
and fusible interfacing. Interfacing
is not required for the small skate,.
Transfer the pattern, embroider the
rose as shown on page 4 and position
as shown in the pattern.

Iron the fusible interfacing onto
the wrong side of the fabric, place
the fabric and lining on top of each
other with printed sides facing and

edges lined up, then sew the top
edge, see Figure A. Fold out the other
piece, line up the two pieces and sew
around. Leave an opening in the
lining pieces, see Figure B.

Cut off excess seam allowance and
turn the whole skate inside out. Stuff
the lining inside the skate. Fold down
a wide edge, marked by a dashed
line in the pattern, so that the lining
shows. Iron the skate. Attach ribbon
to decorate and affix a wire hanging
as described for the Candy Cones
on page 21.

Paint the plywood skate in your
desired colour. Here we have used
'Cappuccino' from the Folk Art
range. Sand the edges with sandpaper
to create a worn, rustic effect.

Sew the plywood skate to the boot
using sewing or embroidery thread in
a suitable colour.

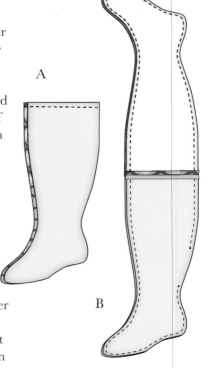

A

B

Angels

Patterns can be found on pages 40–42

YOU WILL NEED
Tilda skin fabric
Fabric for the wings, legs and dress
Tilda hair
Tilda crowns
Brown velvet ribbon to decorate
Stuffing
Decorative sign
Wire (optional)

HOW TO MAKE
BODY
Fold the fabric for the body double and transfer the pattern for one body and two arms for each angel. Fold a piece of light pink fabric double and transfer the pattern for two legs for each angel. Sew around, cut out, fold inside out, iron and stuff all parts with stuffing.

Fold in the seam allowance around the opening in the body, insert the legs and tack in place. Fold in the seam allowance at the opening on the arms, pinch the end and tack the arms under the neck on each side of the body, see Figure A.

DRESS
Fold the fabric for the dress and line up the edges. Transfer the pattern onto the fabric and sew around. Take care not to sew up the openings marked with dashed lines in the pattern.

Cut out the dress, with plenty of seam allowance at the openings. Cut incisions along the seam allowance under the sleeves on each side. Fold over and iron the dress. Cut incisions in the seam allowance around the neck and iron it down. Iron all other seam allowances. Sew brown velvet ribbon around the bottom edge of the dress, stitching the seam allowance at the same time.

Put the dress on the figure. Tack around the opening at the neck and pull tight around the neck, see Figure B. Repeat around each sleeve.

Make the hair and face for the angel as described on page 4.

A

B

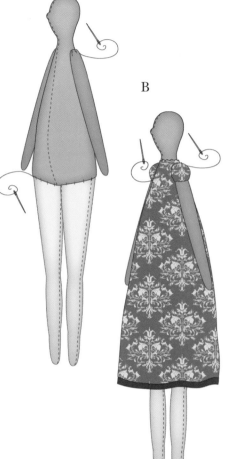

WINGS

Fold the fabric for the wings double and transfer the pattern for a pair of wings for each angel. Sew around the wings, see Figure C. Fold the wings inside out and iron them.

Sew the seams as shown in the pattern, see Figure D. Stuff the wings with stuffing using a wooden stick and stitch the opening closed. Tack the wings onto the figure.

HANGING AND SIGN

Cut a 30cm (12in) piece of wire for each angel. Thread each end through the upper part of the wings to make a hanger. Wind the wire ends back around the wire to fasten, see Figure E.

We recommend using a glue gun to attach the sign and crown. Copy or cut out the sign, as described on page 4, and glue the hands onto each side. Glue the sign and crown in place on the angel.

C

D

E

Gift Boxes

Patterns can be found on pages 35–37

YOU WILL NEED

Decorative card
Double-sided tape
Paper glue
Thin cellophane
Ribbon or brads

HOW TO MAKE

Patterns are available for two sizes of gift boxes. Cut out two of each side from the pattern in your chosen decorative card. Cut out the oval hole in one of the sides, as shown in the pattern. Glue a piece of cellophane over the hole on the inside of the box. Use a ruler and a sharp implement to score along the fold lines of the box, shown with the dashed lines in the pattern.

Glue the four sides together to make a perfect cube, see Figure A. Attach double-sided tape to the edges, fold up the sides and stick together, see Figure B. Make a hole with a hole punch in the top and fasten the lid using a brad or similar. You will need to make two holes if you are using ribbon to close the box.

A
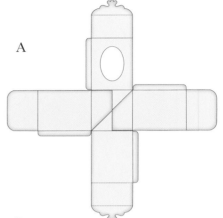

B

GIFTS AND CARDS

A little time spent on Christmas cards and gift-wrapping is always appreciated by the recipient. It's almost like sending a smile, a hug, or a friendly pat on the back. You don't need to add much more, perhaps a beautiful ribbon, a decorative gift tag or a chocolate heart… Here are some ideas for decorations and details.

PAPER HEARTS

Patterns can be found on page 38

Transfer the pattern and cut out double hearts from decorative card. Fold the card in half and use double-sided tape or paper glue on the flap to stick the two heart shapes together. Cut a strip measuring approximately 1.5 x 20cm (⅝ x 8in) for a large heart and 1 x 13cm (⅜ x 5in) for a small heart. Glue the strip on as a hanger. Copy the wings as described on page 4.

Til Anna

HOME

PATTERNS

Add seam allowances to all parts shown in the patterns.
The dashed lines mark openings between two different
fabrics or where two pattern parts should be sewn together.
'ES' stands for extra seam allowance and marks openings
where this is required.
'Double fold' means that the fabric should be folded double
at this line.

ICE SKATE
Fabric x 2
Fusbile interfacing x 2
Lining x 2

Fusible interfacing is
not required for the
small skate.

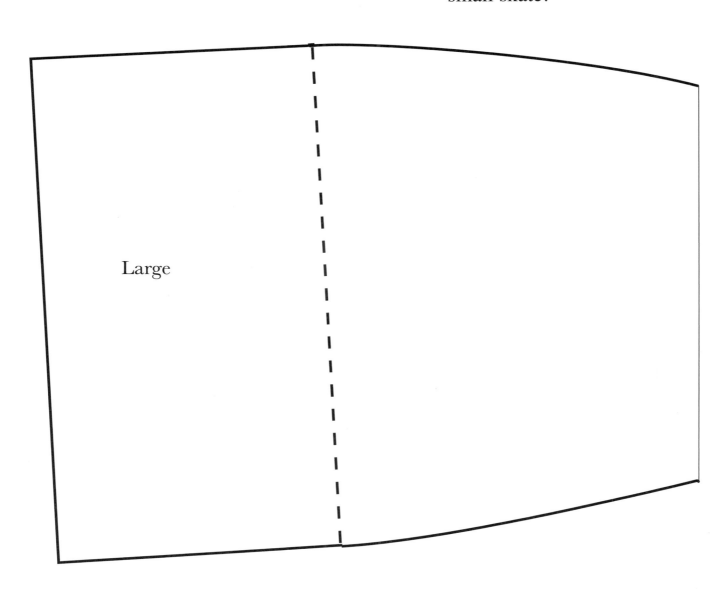

Large

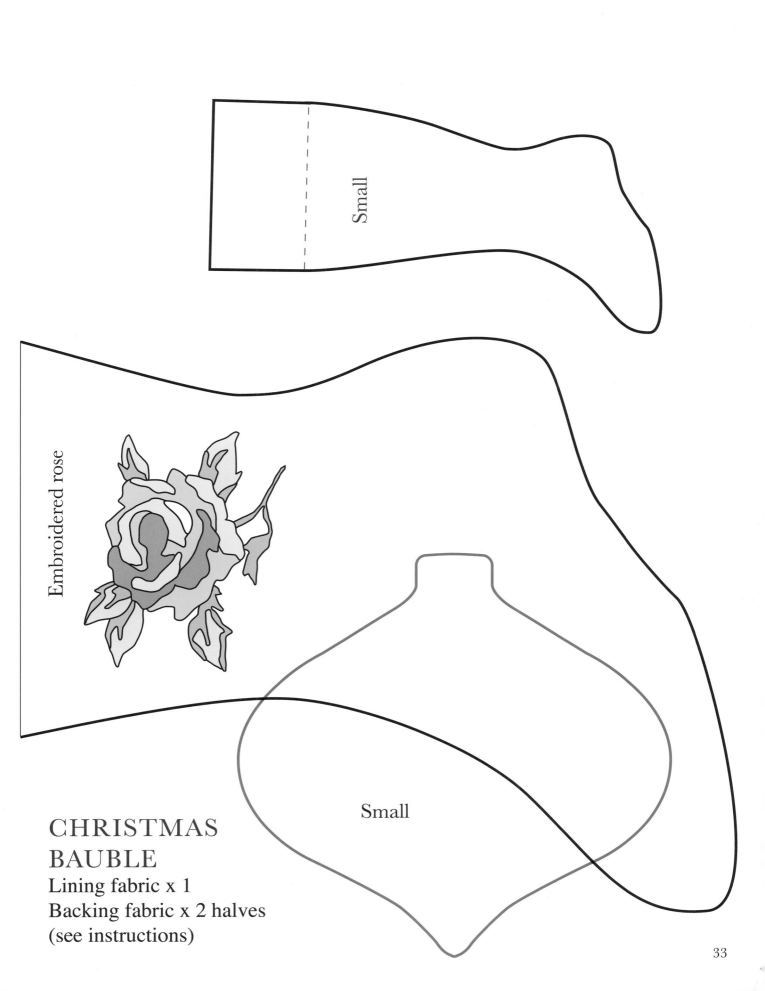

Small

Embroidered rose

Small

CHRISTMAS
BAUBLE
Lining fabric x 1
Backing fabric x 2 halves
(see instructions)

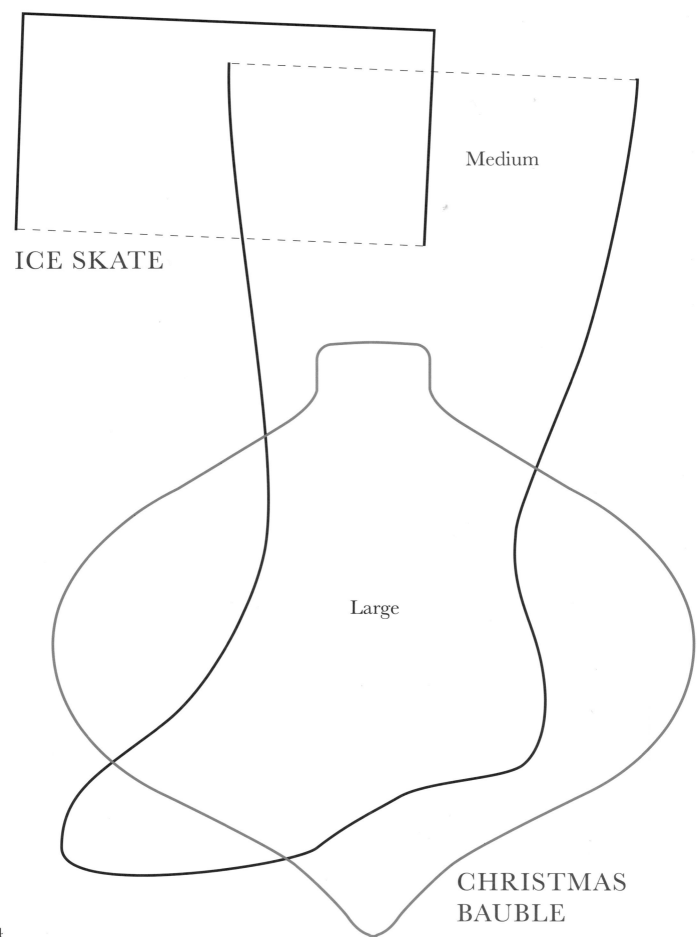

ICE SKATE

Medium

Large

CHRISTMAS
BAUBLE

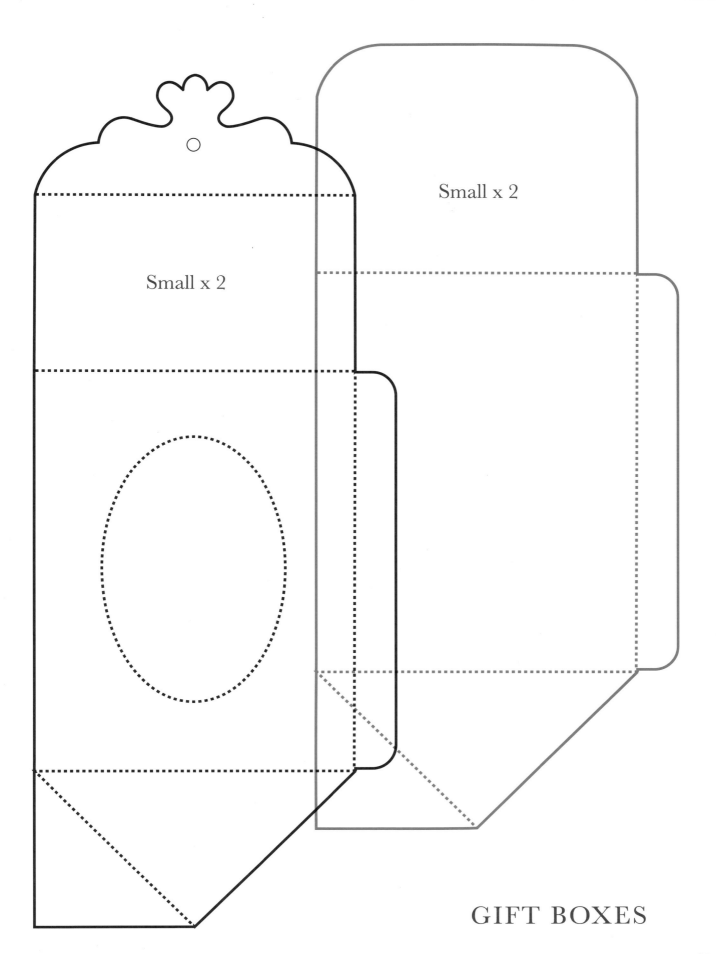

Small x 2

Small x 2

GIFT BOXES

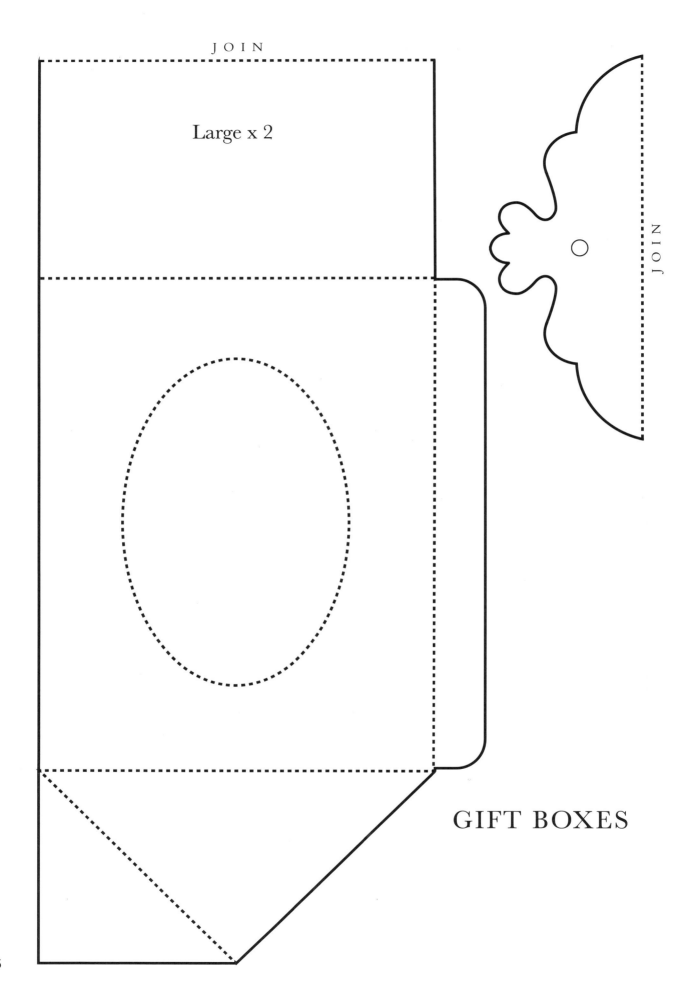

Large x 2

JOIN

JOIN

GIFT BOXES

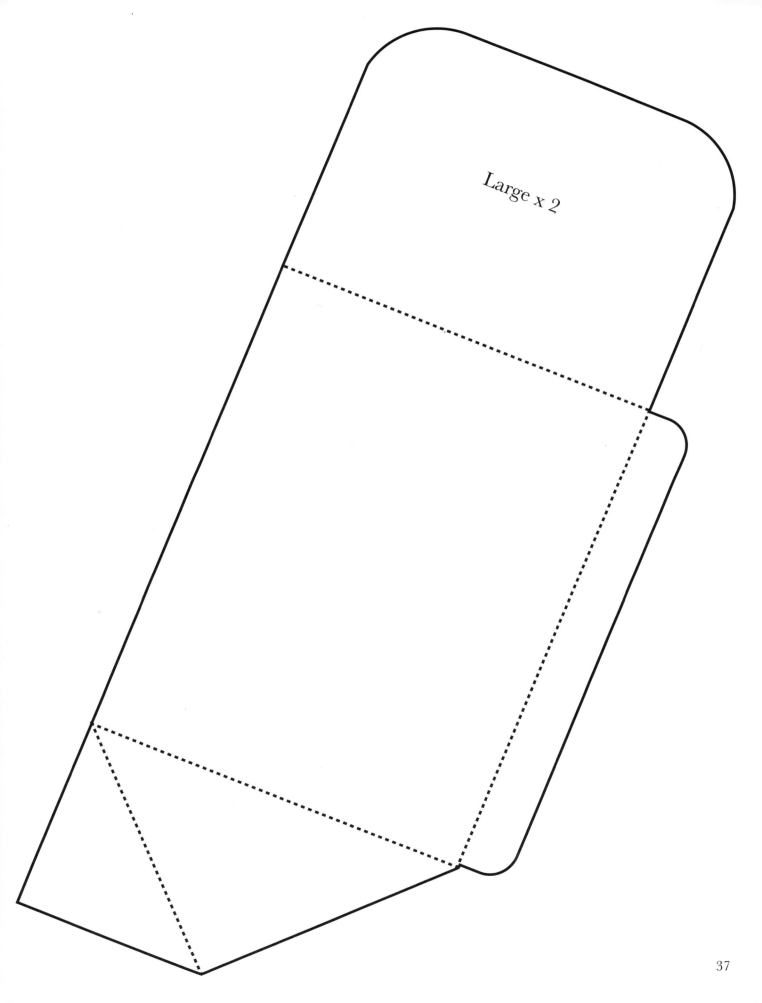

Large x 2

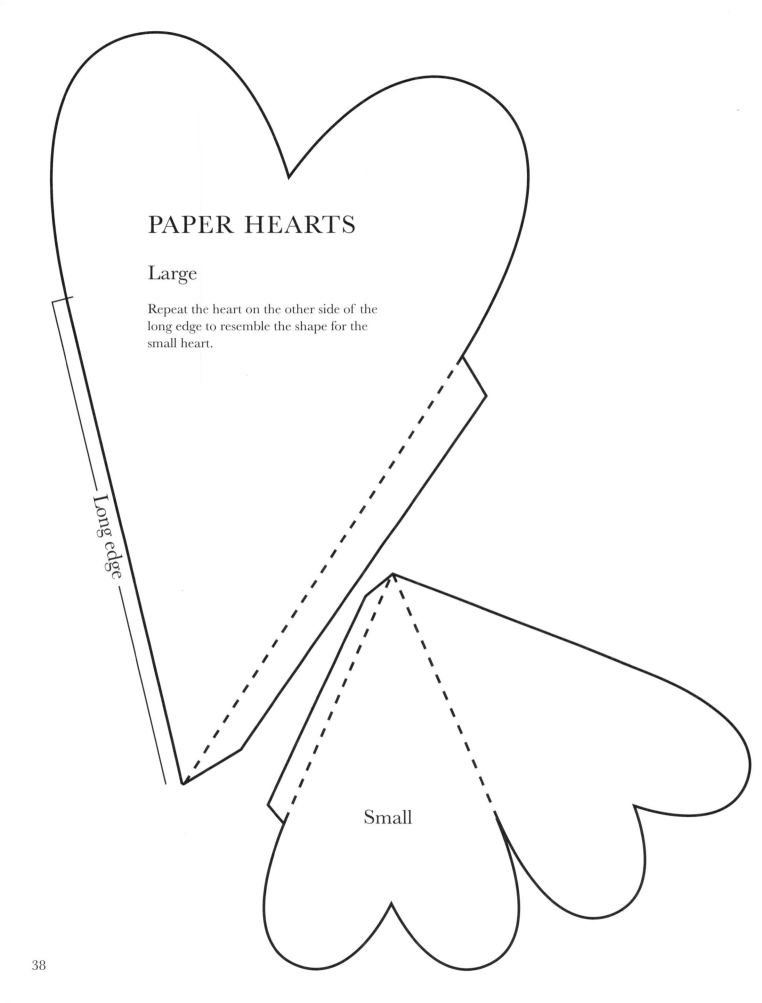

PAPER HEARTS

Large

Repeat the heart on the other side of the long edge to resemble the shape for the small heart.

Long edge

Small

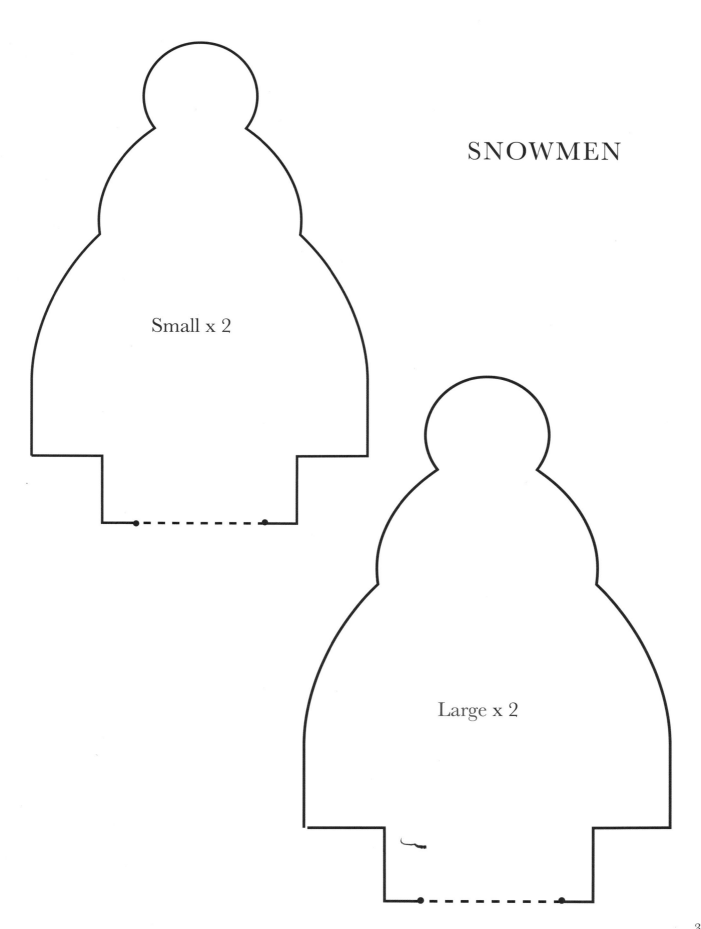

SNOWMEN

Small x 2

Large x 2

ANGELS & PIXIES

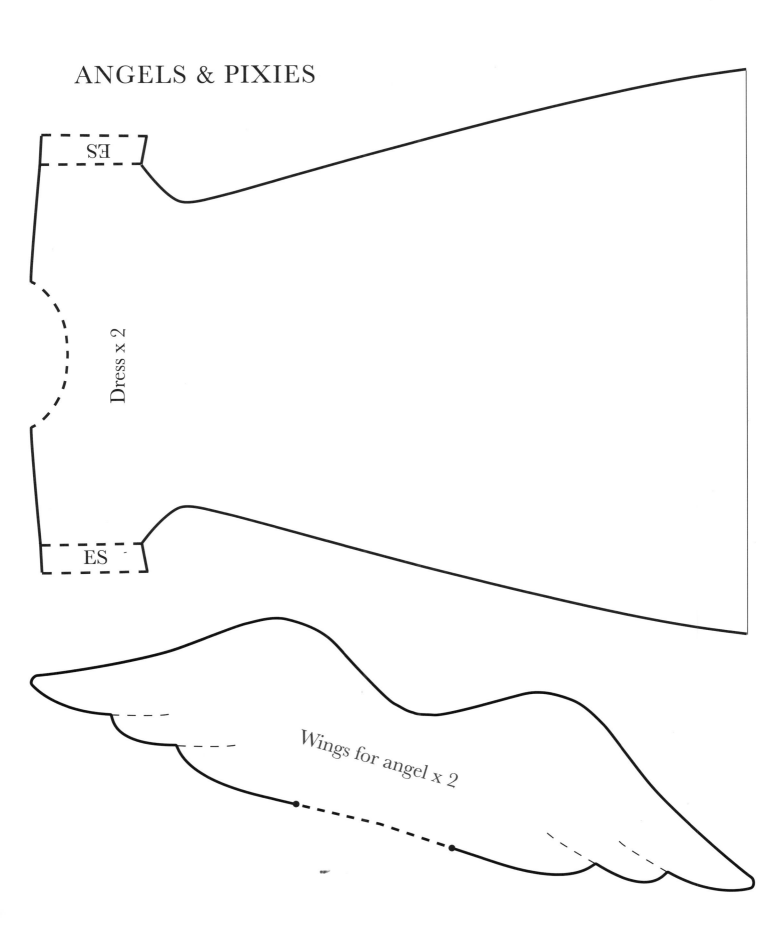

ES

ES

Dress x 2

Wings for angel x 2

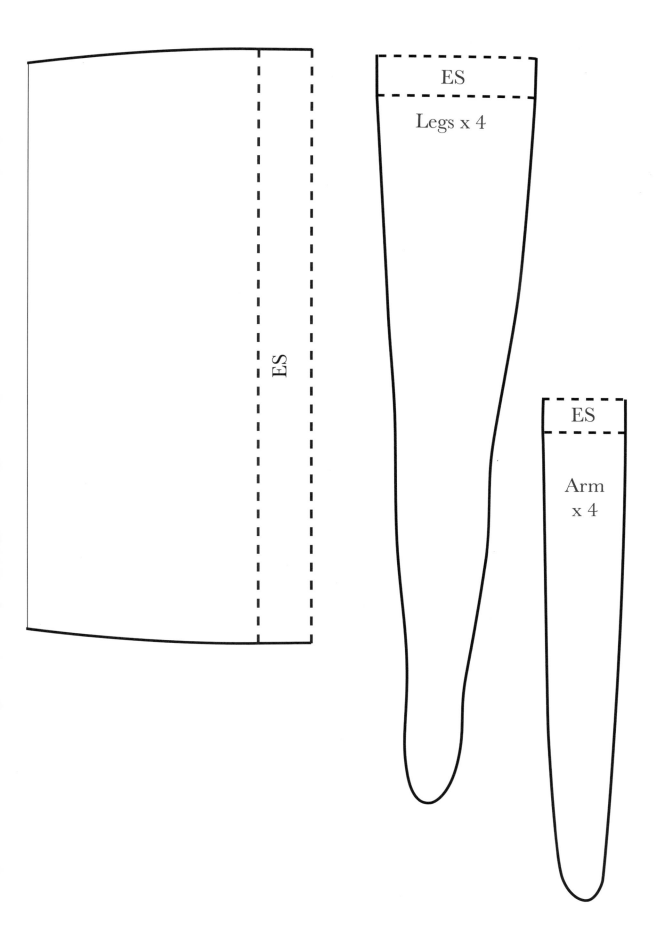

ES

ES

Legs x 4

ES

Arm
x 4

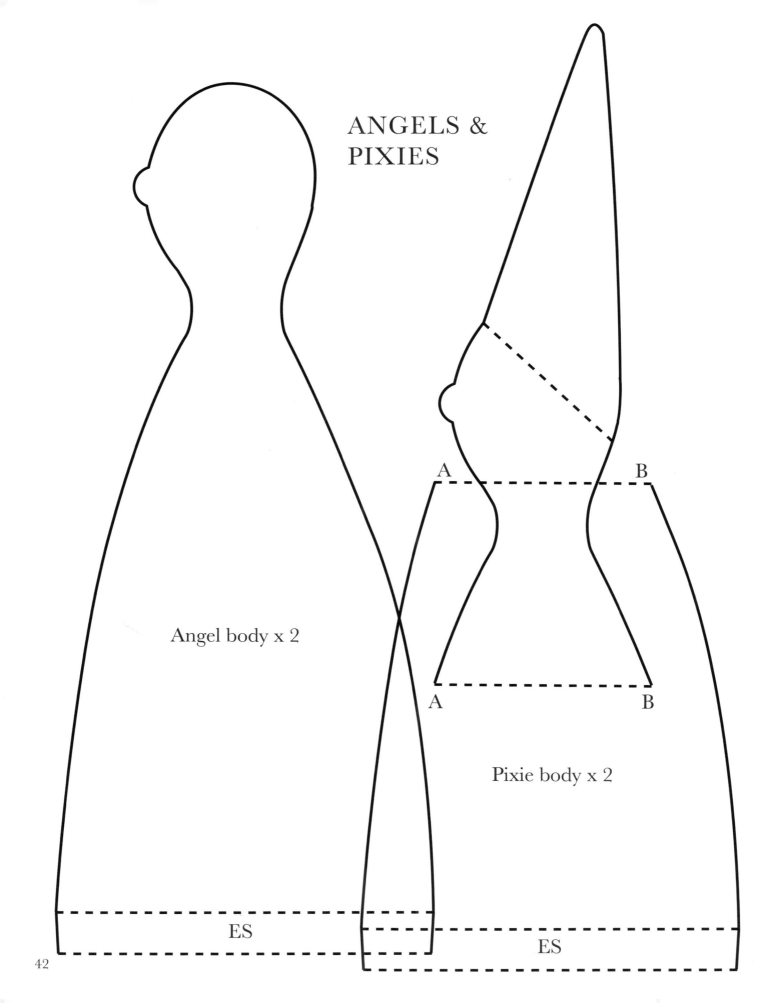

ANGELS &
PIXIES

Angel body x 2

Pixie body x 2

A   B

A   B

ES

ES

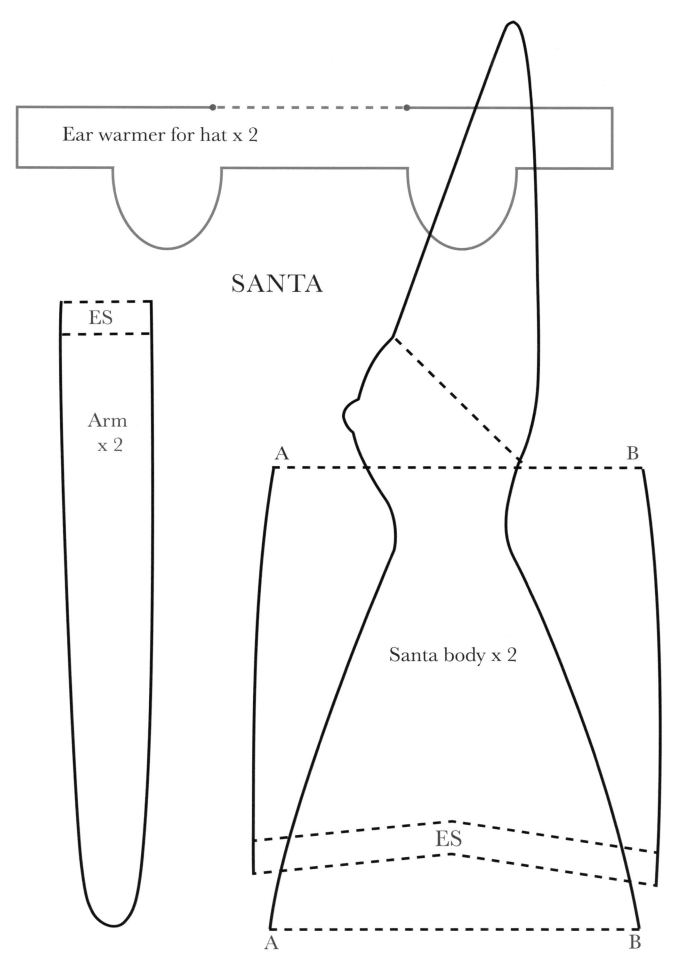

Ear warmer for hat x 2

SANTA

ES

Arm
x 2

A   B

Santa body x 2

ES

A   B

43

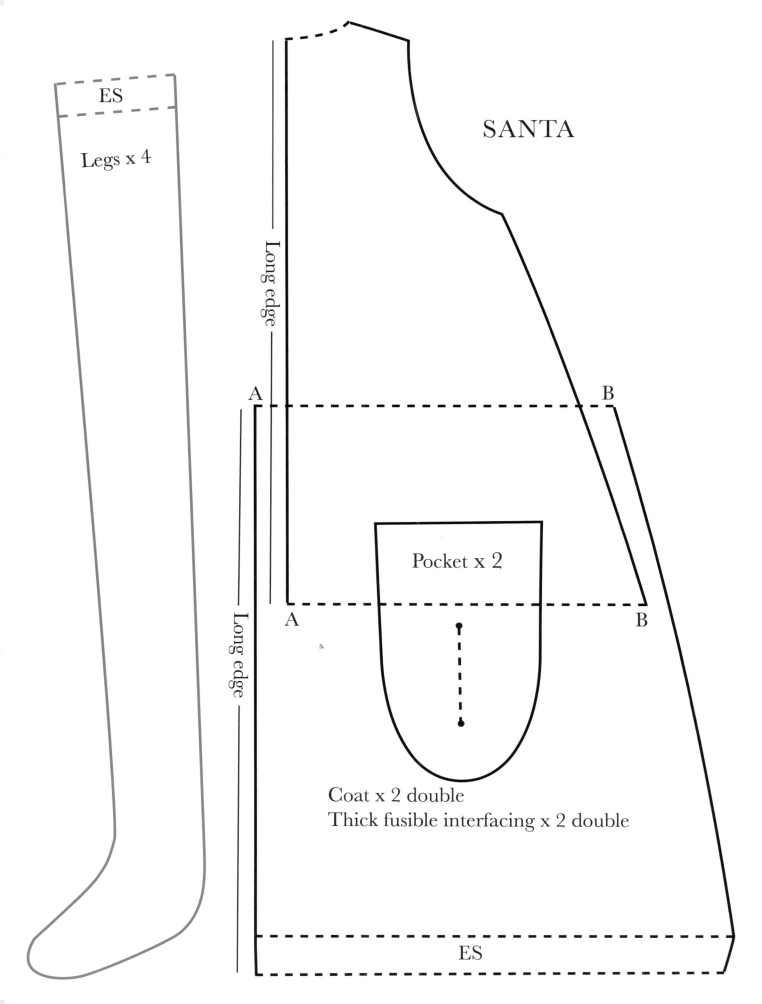

ES

Legs x 4

SANTA

Long edge

A   B

Long edge

Pocket x 2

A   B

Coat x 2 double
Thick fusible interfacing x 2 double

ES

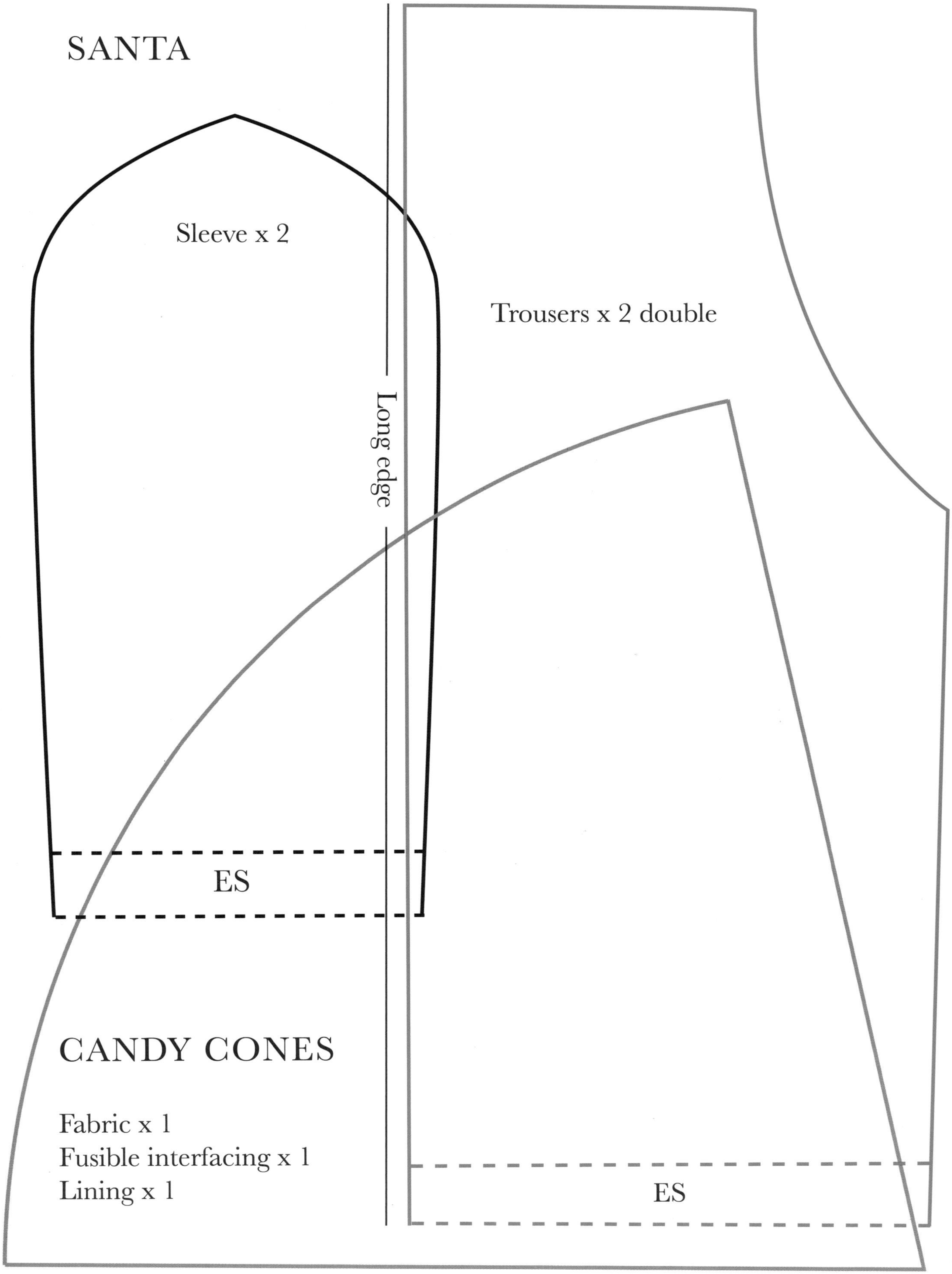

SANTA

Sleeve x 2

Long edge

ES

Trousers x 2 double

ES

CANDY CONES

Fabric x 1
Fusible interfacing x 1
Lining x 1

ACCESSORIES

These accessories can be copied using a photocopier, or scanned and printed as decorations for the projects in this book (170–200 gsm matt photo paper is recommended).

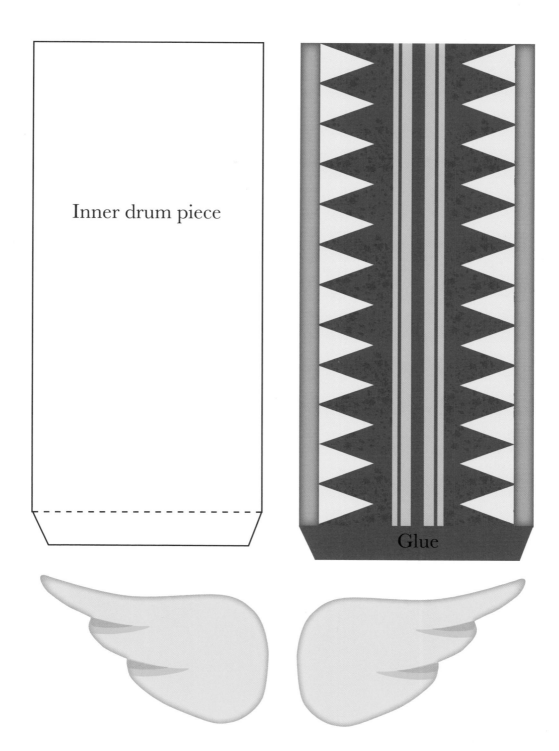

Inner drum piece

Glue

Suppliers

UK

Panduro Hobby
Westway House
Transport Avenue
Brentford
Middlesex TW8 9HF
Tel: 020 8566 1680
trade@panduro.co.uk
www.pandurohobby.co.uk

Coast and Country
Crafts & Quilts
8 Sampson Gardens
Ponsanooth
Truro
Cornwall TR3 7RS
Tel: 01872 863894
www.coastandcountry
crafts.co.uk

Fred Aldous Ltd.
37 Lever Street
Manchester M1 1LW
Tel: 08707 517301
www.fredaldous.co.uk

The Fat Quarters
5 Choprell Road
Blackhall Mill
Newcastle NE17 7TN
Tel: 01207 565728
www.thefatquarters.co.uk

The Sewing Bee
52 Hillfoot Street
Dunoon
Argyll PA23 7DT
Tel: 01369 706879
www.thesewingbee.co.uk

Puddlecrafts
7 St. Clair Park
Route Militaire
St. Sampson
Guernsey GY2 4DX
Tel: 01481 245441
www.puddlecrafts.co.uk

Threads and Patches
48 Aylesbury Street
Fenny Stratford
Bletchley
Milton Keynes
MK2 2BU
Tel: 01908 649687
www.threadsand
patches.co.uk

USA

Coats and Clark USA
PO Box 12229
Greenville
SC29612-0229
Tel: 0800 648 1479
www.coatsandclark.com

Connecting Threads
13118 NE 4th Street
Vancouver
WA 9884
www.connecting
threads.com

eQuilter.com
5455 Spine Road,
Suite E
Boulder
CO 80301
www.equilter.com

Hamels Fabrics
5843 Lickman Road
Chilliwack
British Columbia
V2R 4B5
www.hamelsfabrics.com

Keepsake Quilting
Box 1618 Center
Harbor
NH 03226
www.keepsake
quilting.com

The Craft Connection
21055 Front Street
PO Box 1088
Onley
VA 23418
www.craftconn.com

Index